1001 Things It Means to Be a Mom

(The Good, the Bad, and the Smelly)

by

HARRY H. HARRISON JR.

THOMAS NELSON
Since 1798

NASHVILLE   DALLAS   MEXICO CITY   RIO DE JANEIRO   BEIJING

Table of Contents

Introduction

"There was nothing funny about Mom. She was always serious. Now Dad—he was hilarious."
KENDALL, AGE 22

I was interviewing daughters about their moms when Kendall made this comment. And I was struck by the fact that this lively and precocious twenty-one-year-old didn't know her mother was actually a scream....

Kendall's perception—or misperception—underscores the fact that children do not go to their mothers for laughs. They go for security, hugs, first aid, comfort, forgiveness, money, explanations, instructions, wisdom, help, praise, sympathy, inspiration, protection, and, most of all, love. Well, maybe food too.

From day one, it's Mom who's most concerned about feeding her baby. Who puts up with tantrums all day in hot grocery-store lines. Who'll spend an hour burping a six-month-old who is screaming in her ear. Who'll fill out preschool applications while breastfeeding.

And it's Mom who'll work for ten hours trying to coax the tiniest smile from her child only to have Dad walk in from a business trip, throw the baby up in the air, elicit screams of delight, hand the baby back to a terrified, exhausted mom, and then walk out of the room.

It's Mom who'll dress like a middle-schooler so her daughter will speak to her. Who'll wear a huge button sporting a picture of her high-school senior. Who'll go without so her son can have everything—only to have him say that she needs to do something with her hair.

Moms are hilarious because they're so serious about what they do for their kids.

Frankly, being a mom means a million different things. This book covers just 1001 of them.

Being a Mom

1. Being a mom means thinking you're the luckiest person in the world.

•

2. Being a mom means being a role model.

•

3. Being a mom means discussing with your husband how you want to raise your kids. Before you even have them.

•

4. Being a mom means being over-protective. It's something genetic.

•

5. Being a mom means passing down traditions.

6. Being a mom means having a life filled with bittersweet moments— like the first day of preschool and high school graduation.

•

7. Being a mom means getting mad that your husband doesn't get upset about the same things you do.

•

8. Being a mom means serving as a personal assistant. Often to people shorter than four feet tall.

•

9. Being a mom means saying, "That's not nice."

10. Being a mom means teaching
that every second of every day
isn't supposed to be fun; that
there are days when rooms
have to be cleaned, dishes
picked up, and the laundry done.

•

11. Being a mom means making
lists and schedules and posting
them all around the house
and on the refrigerator door.

•

12. Being a mom means
keeping a flashlight handy
for looking down throats.

13. Being a mom means knowing you have to respect yourself or else your children won't respect you.

•

14. Being a mom means being a good wife.

•

15. Being a mom means teaching kids to respect themselves.

•

16. Being a mom means being willing to be disliked by your kids.

17. Being a mom means insisting everyone is home for dinner. Because when people eat, they talk. And when they talk, you find out what's going on in the family.

•

18. Being a mom means sometimes not telling your child what you really think of them.

•

19. Being a mom means feeling overwhelmed when your husband is out of town.

•

20. Being a mom is thinking coffee makes you a better mother.

21. Being a mom means learning
how to text-message so you can
communicate with your children.

•

22. Being a mom means suspecting that
your happiness is totally dependent on
the washing machine working.

•

23. Being a mom means making
sure your kids go to the art
museum, the science museum,
and the history museum.

•

24. Being a mom means,
at times, being paranoid about
your children's well-being.

•

25. Being a mom means having
eyes in the back of your head.

•

26. Being a mom means
bragging that your children
are the bright spot of your life.

•

27. Being a mom means
developing a strange fascination
with refrigerator magnets.

•

28. Being a mom means feeling
absolutely certain about your parenting
principles. Until you have kids.

29. Being a mom means taking
a vacation away from the kids.

•

30. Being a mom means
explaining why laundry detergent
doesn't go in the dishwasher.

•

31. Being a mom means
upsetting your child because
you changed your hairdo.

•

32. Being a mom means being
obsessively vigilant the moment you
suddenly realize you are not in control.

33. Being a mom means believing
that kids have no privacy rights.

•

34. Being a mom means always feeling
judged by the mommy police.

•

35. Being a mom means baking
their favorite birthday cake.
Even when they're twenty-five.

•

36. Being a mom means having a
love/hate relationship with McDonald's.

37. Being a mom means needle-pointing personalized Christmas stockings. And telling your husband his old socks won't do.

•

38. Being a mom means making homemade chicken soup when someone gets sick. Even when that someone is eighteen.

•

39. Being a mom means digging stuff out of ears.

•

40. Being a mom means reading books at each stage of your child's development.

41. Being a mom means constantly second-guessing yourself at home even though you have absolutely no trouble making decisions at the office.

•

42. Being a mom means cooking dinner while everyone else is watching TV.

•

43. Being a mom means feeling as if you were treated like a rock star with your first baby and like a groupie with the second.

44. Being a mom means
checking your children for
head lice. Even adult children.

•

45. Being a mom means telling
everyone you don't need help
in the kitchen—and then getting
upset because no one helps you.

•

46. Being a mom means
being told, "Don't tell Dad."

•

47. Being a mom means asking yourself
every time you read a newspaper,
"What if that had been my child?"

48. Being a mom means not being able
to look at pictures of starving children.

•

49. Being a mom means moving
to a neighborhood where you see
sidewalks and baby toys outside.

•

50. Being a mom means needing
a manicure in the worst way.

•

51. Being a mom means
keeping your relationship
with your husband a priority.

52. Being a mom means feeling like you don't spend enough time with your children. Even if you don't work outside of the home.

•

53. Being a mom means finding yourself strangely against war.

•

54. Being a mom means planning family vacations for the next fifty years.

•

55. Being a mom means knowing which restaurants within a fifty-mile radius let kids eat free. And provide crayons and coloring placemats.

56. Being a mom means reading parenting magazines to see if writers without kids know something about child raising you don't.

•

57. Being a mom means trying to figure out how much privacy to give your child at each stage of their life. And never feeling like you're doing it right.

•

58. Being a mom means getting up off your deathbed to clean the house, because what would people think if they saw that your house was a mess?

59. Being a mom means
continually trying to figure out
what's important to your child.

•

60. Being a mom means
knowing you need friends to talk to,
because you can only have so many
conversations with people three feet tall.

•

61. Being a mom means bribing
your kids as soon as they can talk.

•

62. Being a mom means looking
all winter long for a summer camp.

63. Being a mom means realizing that managing a 100,000-person company is child's play compared to managing two toddlers.

•

64. Being a mom means shopping for the perfect end-of-the-season gift for your child's coach.

•

65. Being a mom means hearing, "You don't trust me" and thinking, *Well, yes, that's probably true.*

•

66. Being a mom means letting everyone know you'd better receive touching and meaningful Mother's Day cards and gifts.

67. Being a mom means keeping every Mother's Day card in a special box and rereading them year after year.

•

68. Being a mom means actually feeling excited over the prospect of a horde of four-year-olds invading your home for a birthday party.

•

69. Being a mom means trying to create the best learning experience for your child every single day— and feeling guilty when you don't.

70. Being a mom means treating all your children the same and still being accused of playing favorites.

•

71. Being a mom means saying, "When I was your age…"

•

72. Being a mom means trying to stage a Christmas card photo and hoping this year everyone will be happy, clean, and not hitting each other.

•

73. Being a mom means anguishing after you've had a fight with your kids— no matter how much in the right you are.

74. Being a mom means
paying more for the sitter than
for what your night out cost.

•

75. Being a mom means continually
balancing what you know is best for your
children with wanting them to be happy.

•

76. Being a mom means
developing "the look" that will
stop misbehavior in its tracks.

•

77. Being a mom means hugging your child
after a fight. Even if he or she is still mad.

78. Being a mom means knowing where the birth certificates are.

•

79. Being a mom means being shocked at the PG-13 movie you're watching with your kids.

•

80. Being a mom means trying to tell your child—in a motherly, kind, and loving way—they look like a weirdo.

•

81. Being a mom means wondering if your kids have heard anything you've said to them in their entire lives.

82. Being a mom means insisting
that piano lessons be worked
into the family budget.

•

83. Being a mom means
intuitively knowing when
your child has had a hard day.

•

84. Being a mom means constantly saying,
"I love you," because that's the most
important thing a child needs to know.

•

85. Being a mom means never
dismissing a child's fears and worries.

86. Being a mom means saying, "You can't do anything without me finding out about it"— and hoping they still believe you even when they're twenty.

•

87. Being a mom means knowing there are some things kids find difficult to talk about. But finding a way to get them talking anyway.

•

88. Being a mom means always being on your child's side.

89. Being a mom means
stressing the importance of
responsibility and maturity.

•

90. Being a mom means feeling like you
have to throw fabulous parties for
your kids—and then learning years
later that they don't remember
a single one before eighth grade.

•

91. Being a mom means wanting
your children to have a relationship
with their grandparents.

92. Being a mom means hiring a nanny—and then worrying if you can trust her. Then installing a nanny cam. Then realizing that if you record eight hours daily, you have to somehow watch the eight hours of tape.

•

93. Being a mom means knowing the fat, sodium, carbohydrate, and calorie counts of a frozen macaroni-and-cheese dinner. And happily serving it anyway.

•

94. Being a mom means knowing boys and girls should be treated equally. But differently.

95. Being a mom means introducing your children to the mystical wonder of Christmas lights. Year after year.

•

96. Being a mom means making your kids kiss you goodnight. Every night. No matter how late they come in.

•

97. Being a mom means finding that your child has, without warning, suddenly graduated from college and is in executive training.

98. Being a mom means worrying you won't be able to stand the person your "baby" marries.

•

99. Being a mom means developing the uncanny ability to make it all better.

•

100. Being a mom means worrying that you've become your mother.

Pregnant Moms

101. Being a mom means realizing that perhaps the greatest gift in life is a baby.

•

102. Being a mom means having an earthquake jolt your life.

•

103. Being a mom means tearing up while cooking oatmeal. (Hormones are in play.)

•

104. Being a mom means realizing pregnancy isn't a severe medical condition. It's a miracle.

•

105. Being a mom means panicking that you might have just gotten mercury poisoning from eating swordfish.

106. Being a mom means worrying you've waited too late in life to have children. Or started too early.

•

107. Being a mom means headaches, stomachaches, heartaches, and exhaustion. And loving it all.

•

108. Being a mom means having your heart stop when you see the first ultrasound of your baby.

•

109. Being a mom means marveling over your fuller breasts.

110. Being a mom means wondering why morning sickness is called morning sickness since the only time you throw up is in the afternoon.

111. Being a mom means listening to your husband have morning sickness too—and wanting to shoot him. (Sympathy pains are weird.)

•

112. Being a mom means thinking you'll look and feel much better if you cut off all your hair.

113. Being a mom means asking strangers in the grocery store for the name of a good pediatrician.

•

114. Being a mom means explaining to your husband what a pediatrician is.

•

115. Being a mom means deciding that even though you're pregnant, nauseous, and tired, you're going to start an exercise program for the sake of your baby's health.

•

116. Being a mom means taking a pregnancy yoga class.

117. Being a mom means realizing that even in the most expensive maternity clothes, you still look way pregnant.

•

118. Being a mom means fleeing a restaurant when someone three tables over lights up a cigarette.

•

119. Being a mom means wanting to somehow name your child after your parents and the father's parents—and work in something new and unique.

120. Being a mom means not reacting when your husband says he likes the name "Montana" whether the baby is a boy or a girl.

•

121. Being a mom means rejecting a name for your baby because a person with that name picked on you in grade school.

•

122. Being a mom means worrying your favorite name is too popular and could hinder your child's happiness and admission into medical school.

123. Being a mom is hiring
a naming consultant and having
them come up with Bubba.

•

124. Being a mom means buying
a book of 100,000 baby names—
and then naming your baby
after your grandmother.

•

125. Being a mom is worrying
you'll have name remorse. And realizing
your mother thinks you're losing it.

126. Being a mom means calling
the baby by its name while
it's still in your womb and even
introducing it by name to strangers.

•

127. Being a mom means praying for
your baby by its name before it's born.

•

128. Being a mom means
ordering a Perrier instead of
a daiquiri. And not complaining.

•

129. Being a mom means driving past
Starbucks even though your eyes are
glued together from being up all night.

130. Being a mom means having people say inappropriate things to you. Sometimes even other moms don't know what to say to a pregnant woman.

•

131. Being a mom means deciding that the whole "pregnancy glow" thing is a myth—created by men.

•

132. Being a mom means forgetting why you're standing in the grocery store. In pregnancy, memory goes as fast as your body does.

133. Being a mom means having this overwhelming craving for mustard soup.

•

134. Being a mom means giving up Diet Coke.

•

135. Being a mom means having your husband tell you that you're starting to snore.

•

136. Being a mom means having complete strangers want to touch your stomach.

137. Being a mom means realizing your husband has three things going against him: 1. He's scared witless. 2. He doesn't know what to say or do. 3. He's a man.

•

138. Being a mom means realizing that you're carrying God's child.

•

139. Being a mom means seriously looking at the neighborhood's nine-year-old girls as prospective baby-sitters.

•

140. Being a mom means lying down on the floor in an expensive restaurant because you're dizzy. And not thinking twice about it.

141. Being a mom means praying
not only for your newborn
but also for the husband or wife
God has picked for your child
twenty-five years or so from now.

•

142. Being a mom means reading
every pregnancy book ever written
while your husband is playing golf.

•

143. Being a mom means feeling
inexplicably sexy even though
you're growing larger every day.

144. Being a mom means having a little foot wedged up in your ribs right about the time your husband gets frisky.

•

145. Being a mom means worrying that if you don't bank the umbilical cord blood, your baby will be at risk even though experts say it's extremely rare that people ever need their cord blood.

•

146. Being a mom means having your husband rub your stomach until your baby starts kicking, then being kept awake all night while he rolls over and goes to sleep.

147. Being a mom means questioning why
medical science has failed to improve
iron supplements in the last century.

•

148. Being a mom means maintaining
regular exercise when a man would
have stopped two months ago.

•

149. Being a mom means calculating
that you have some forty weeks
for something to go wrong.

•

150. Being a mom means finding
dark splotches on your face and
body that didn't used to be there.

151. Being a mom means doing stretching exercises at 2:00 a.m. because your legs are restless and cramping.

•

152. Being a mom means not believing your husband is sexually attracted to you at nine months— and then deciding it's proof that all men are animals.

•

153. Being a mom means sleeping against a wall because you're too big to lie down.

154. Being a mom means worrying your husband will forget where the hospital is when it matters most.

•

155. Being a mom means succumbing to the urge to turn the übercool media room into a pink nursery with rainbows and unicorns.

•

156. Being a mom means fretting over whether to use cloth diapers versus disposables, when the same fate awaits both.

•

157. Being a mom means realizing the Lamaze classes are designed to keep your husband occupied while you deliver the baby.

158. Being a mom means feeling too nauseated to do anything but eat a pan of brownies.

•

159. Being a mom means explaining to the first child what a blessing the second one will be when it's clear he doesn't believe you.

•

160. Being a mom means having a support group. A loving husband is ideal, but friends and relatives can do a lot to help too.

161. Being a mom means
feeling like you have no idea what
you're doing despite all the books,
your mother, your friends who
are mothers, and your in-laws.

•

162. Being a mom means strategically
plotting bathroom stops.

•

163. Being a mom means realizing
that now's the time to stop drinking
alcohol. Not cut down. Stop.

•

164. Being a mom means giving
up smoking even if it means
you're chewing out the mailman.

165. Being a mom means staying up all hours of the night reading about the pros and cons of breast-feeding versus bottle-feeding.

•

166. Being a mom means breaking down in tears upon hearing stories of sick babies.

•

167. Being a mom means worrying about money—and then ordering birth announcements that cost $500.

168. Being a mom means discovering the baby crib you loved in the store comes delivered in two million pieces—and doesn't include the mattress or bedding.

•

169. Being a mom means teaching your baby the sound of your voice while he's still in the womb.

•

170. Being a mom means if you're not eating, the baby you're carrying is not eating.

•

171. Being a mom means decorating your nursery at 2:00 a.m.

172. Being a mom means thinking
you need to buy everything now,
forgetting the stores will still
be open after the baby is born.

•

173. Being a mom means feeling
sure that the ninth month of
pregnancy is the worst thing that
can ever happen to your body.

•

174. Being a mom means thinking
seriously about breast-feeding
because it can save some $2500
a year on formula and supplies.

175. Being a mom means explaining to your husband why a baby stroller costs as much as a used car.

•

176. Being a mom means praying you're making the right decision about vaccinations.

•

177. Being a mom means forgetting how much you love your husband while you're in the throes of labor and holding him accountable for your stomach almost bursting.

178. Being a mom means forgiving your husband if he faints during delivery.

•

179. Being a mom means declaring you don't want the epidural— and then screaming at the nurse, "Give me the *%#&@* shot!"

•

180. Being a mom means showing off your cesarean scar.

Baby Moms

181. Being a mom means learning
what an inflatable donut is all about.

•

182. Being a mom means realizing
the relationship between you and
your husband has just changed.

•

183. Being a mom means feeling terrified
when you bring your baby home.

•

184. Being a mom means being
blindsided by love for your baby,
but still worrying you don't love her
as much as books say you should.

185. Being a mom means
worrying you'll forget everything
you learned in your baby-care class.

•

186. Being a mom means having
major surgery like a C-section, but
giving yourself two hours to recover.

•

187. Being a mom means feeling
as if you've won the lottery the first
time you successfully burp your baby.

•

188. Being a mom means telling
people to bring food when they
ask how they can help you.

189. Being a mom means realizing you suddenly have psychotic hair.

•

190. Being a mom means nudging your husband at 3:00 a.m. to get up and deal with the screaming baby.

•

191. Being a mom means counting your baby's stools and wanting to share this information with your husband.

•

192. Being a mom means sometimes questioning why you decided to have a baby.

193. Being a mom means thinking if your husband ever touches you again, you'll cut his hand off.

•

194. Being a mom means knowing what postpartum depression is and that, at its first sign, you should call the doctor.

•

195. Being a mom means knowing exactly what a four-week, five-day, eleven-hour-old girl should weigh.

•

196. Being a mom means learning too late that the most toxic places in the world are not nuclear dumps, but pediatricians' offices.

197. Being a mom means feeling total bliss over a little grin.

•

198. Being a mom means finding hair in places it never grew before.

•

199. Being a mom means assuming you know more about parenting than the father does.

200. Being a mom means getting kicked while changing a diaper—and not reacting.

201. Being a mom means
being unable to imagine
living one day without your
newborn baby by your side.

•

202. Being a mom means knowing
in advance your baby will go through
5,000 diapers—and wondering,
"Do I wash them, throw them away,
or send them out for cleaning?"

•

203. Being a mom means looking
forward to Mommy & Me classes.

204. Being a mom means
asking the pediatrician for
samples of disposable diapers,
formula, and skin cream. Fearlessly.

•

205. Being a mom means discovering a
well of patience you never knew existed.

•

206. Being a mom means not understanding why your husband would rather watch
TV than discuss diaper brands.

•

207. Being a mom means reading
ten blogs before you clip your baby's
fingernails for the first time.

208. Being a mom means suddenly thinking more about your own childhood. And marveling at how your mom did it.

•

209. Being a mom means giving your baby a stuffed toy— and ten months later worrying what to do when it falls apart.

•

210. Being a mom means holding a baby in one arm and groceries in the other.

•

211. Being a mom means dreading two words: ear infection.

212. Being a mom means reciting
the alphabet. Over and over.

•

213. Being a mom means taking
your baby to the doctor because of this
weird thing on her thumb, only to learn
it's a callus caused by sucking her thumb.

•

214. Being a mom means worrying how to
keep your baby safe in an unsafe world.

•

215. Being a mom means accepting you're
going to show up late sometimes. In fact,
people are lucky you show up at all.

216. Being a mom means thinking if the baby store stocks it, you must have it.

•

217. Being a mom means convincing the cranky nurse at the pediatrician's office that your child is the sickest three-month-old on the planet.

•

218. Being a mom means holding, rocking, and swaying a baby who's screaming in your face at 100 decibels— and doing so for hours. (That's equivalent to the noise of a jackhammer.)

219. Being a mom means finding
the remains of a pacifier
in your washing machine.

•

220. Being a mom means
worrying about your baby's
birthmark even though
80 percent of babies have them.

•

221. Being a mom means asking your
waiter to heat your baby's bottle for you.

•

222. Being a mom means
finding stretch marks where
there used to be smooth, sexy skin.

223. Being a mom means
calling the pediatrician at 3:00 a.m.
because the baby's stool is green.

•

224. Being a mom means explaining
to your husband why your baby
needs to sleep in your bed at night.

•

225. Being a mom means worrying
your six-month-old will fall behind
if you don't buy him flashcards.

•

226. Being a mom means getting
punched and kicked in bed by your
baby and telling yourself how sweet it is.

227. Being a mom means crying when your husband says, "From now on, the baby sleeps in the crib."

•

228. Being a mom means being able to change a diaper with your eyes closed.

•

229. Being a mom means not taking medication because you are breast-feeding.

•

230. Being a mom means thinking the inventor of the rocking chair should be given the Nobel Peace Prize.

231. Being a mom means knowing, by the sound of your baby's screams, when it's time to call the doctor.

•

232. Being a mom means becoming an instant nutritionist by building a customized food plan for your child at http://www.mypyramid.gov/.

•

233. Being a mom means realizing your schedule means absolutely nothing to your baby.

234. Being a mom means expecting your child's doctor to work twenty-four hours a day, seven days a week, including holidays, and especially the days your baby is sick.

•

235. Being a mom means learning a new language of initials, like MMR, DtaP, and Hib.

•

236. Being a mom means leaving the doctor's office in a panic after your baby gets vaccinated because her crying makes you want to cry.

237. Being a mom means waiting at the front door for your husband to get home so you can hand the baby to him and go take a shower.

•

238. Being a mom means realizing the most important person in your pediatrician's office is the scheduling nurse. So you bring her gifts.

•

239. Being a mom means catching your baby's flu virus. Only you're sicker. And there's no one to take care of you.

240. Being a mom means talking to your baby all the time. Because this is how he'll learn to talk.

•

241. Being a mom means forgetting a baby will impact your career, your savings, and your retirement.

•

242. Being a mom means strapping a colicky baby in a car seat at 2:00 a.m. and driving around the block twenty-seven times in an effort to lull him to sleep.

243. Being a mom means trading in your purse for a diaper bag.

•

244. Being a mom means measuring your baby's life in days, then weeks, then months...

•

245. Being a mom means living in a different-smelling world.

•

246. Being a mom means loving naptime more than your baby does.

247. Being a mom means
not crying over spilled milk,
but cleaning it up—for years.

•

248. Being a mom means realizing
all moms are going through the
exact same things—except the
thin moms who have nannies.

•

249. Being a mom means realizing that
no alarm can match your baby's shriek.

•

250. Being a mom means trying to
stuff baby food into a tiny mouth that
snaps shut at the approach of a spoon.

251. Being a mom means
not understanding how anyone
could consider an abortion.

•

252. Being a mom means putting
whiskey on your baby's gums
to ease teething pain—and then
panicking at the thought that you're
turning your baby into an alcoholic.

•

253. Being a mom means talking
endlessly with other moms about
teething, and burping, and rolling
over, and the color of poop.

254. Being a mom means feeling like "doing nothing" is vastly underrated.

•

255. Being a mom means wondering how you could ever be apart from your baby all day long.

•

256. Being a mom means realizing cloth diapers are environmentally friendly to everything but your home environment.

•

257. Being a mom is not noticing the smelly diaper hamper while your husband keeps air freshener on his bedside table.

258. Being a mom means learning when babies sleep more, they eat more.

•

259. Being a mom means developing a need for a camcorder, a digital camera, a color printer, and a new big-screen TV so that you can watch and record everything about your baby.

•

260. Being a mom means carrying scented bags for dirty diapers.

•

261. Being a mom means worrying your breasts won't hold enough milk to satisfy your baby.

262. Being a mom means
buying clothes at Target instead
of Neiman's or Nordstrom's.

•

263. Being a mom means changing your
baby's diaper in a restaurant while the
diners sitting around you are gagging.

•

264. Being a mom means
learning the hard way that
boys tend to spray straight up.

•

265. Being a mom means praying
over your child while she sleeps.

266. Being a mom means
needing to shower, vacuum, wash
clothes, change the baby, make lunch,
and take a nap—all at the same time.

•

267. Being a mom means storing
all the clothes your baby grows out of
because you just might have another.

•

268. Being a mom means finding
tiny socks all over the house.

•

269. Being a mom means your
clothes get wet from being gummed.

270. Being a mom means setting
a schedule for bedtimes, naps,
meals, and baths. And sticking to it.

•

271. Being a mom means not being
aware your husband is freaked out
about money, living space, responsibilities, and your constant exhaustion.

•

272. Being a mom means
thinking the baby milestone
chart is dumb—unless your baby
is four months ahead of schedule.
Then it's something to brag about.

273. Being a mom means sleeping when the baby sleeps—or else not sleeping at all.

•

274. Being a mom means bronzing your baby's first pair of shoes—and then having no idea what to do with them.

•

275. Being a mom means giving your child a special soft and wonderful blanket to help him sleep better. And putting it on his bed for the next fifteen years.

•

276. Being a mom means exhaustion is a normal state of being.

277. Being a mom means being able to converse with an engineer about the design, installation, and safety rating of different car seats.

•

278. Being a mom means forgetting you left a dirty diaper on your friend's patio.

•

279. Being a mom means getting showered, dressed, and made up in one-tenth the time it used to take.

•

280. Being a mom means assuming complete strangers want to hear about the color of your baby's poop.

281. Being a mom means trying
not to care what other mothers think
of your clothes, your baby's clothes,
or your baby's development.

•

282. Being a mom means
obsessing about your child's
birthday parties while your
husband wanders around saying,
"What's the big deal?"

•

283. Being a mom means
not remembering when you
weren't changing diapers.

284. Being a mom means
having diaper wipes stuffed in your
purse, pockets, car doors, glove
compartment, and kitchen drawers.

•

285. Being a mom means feeling
ecstatic one second—and then feeling
overwhelmed, lonely, or fearful the next.

•

286. Being a mom means feeling
guilty about using disposable diapers
instead of cloth. But using them anyway.

•

287. Being a mom means agreeing
to pay a suspicious-looking teenager
$25 so you can take a nap.

288. Being a mom means knowing a baby's first question is "What does it taste like?"

•

289. Being a mom means reading to your child every day, beginning at six months of age.

•

290. Being a mom means standing naked in front of the mirror to see if your body is in there somewhere.

•

291. Being a mom means staying up all night listening to the baby monitor.

292. Being a mom means
showing pictures of your child
to people standing in line with
you in the grocery store.

•

293. Being a mom means
remembering when you used
to have time to read novels.

•

294. Being a mom means wanting
to throw yourself on top of your
baby when anyone with a runny
nose or hacking cough is anywhere
remotely near your zip code.

295. Being a mom means rubbing your hands and your baby's with antibacterial soap five times a day.

•

296. Being a mom means deciding that stretch marks are a badge of courage.

•

297. Being a mom means denying to your husband you smell a dirty diaper.

•

298. Being a mom means wondering how in the world you could love someone so much.

299. Being a mom means assuming your friends want to hear all about your baby's constipation issues.

•

300. Being a mom means stocking most of the baby's nursery into a diaper bag— and then realizing you can't carry it.

•

301. Being a mom means dressing your baby as if you lived in the North Pole when the temperature is in the sixties.

•

302. Being a mom means ending a vacation after seven hours because you miss your baby—even though you paid for three days. In advance.

303. Being a mom means realizing you now have a new identity, even if you were once editor of *Vogue*.

•

304. Being a mom means posting stories about your baby's pooping issues on the Internet not thinking you'll have to explain this to him eighteen years from now.

•

305. Being a mom means airing out your bedroom because the baby's diaper leaked all over the bed.

306. Being a mom means signing up for weekly e-mails from www.BabyCenter.com.

•

307. Being a mom means thinking you can prevent diaper rash.

•

308. Being a mom means dealing with a one-year-old who'll eat only fruit and goldfish.

•

309. Being a mom means developing the uncanny ability to express milk while driving to work.

310. Being a mom means seriously considering a $10,000 pacifier consultant because your baby doesn't seem to do it right.

•

311. Being a mom means trying to be sexy with pureed carrot-crusted hair.

•

312. Being a mom means feeling as if your financial situation hovers between precarious and disastrous.

313. Being a mom means learning that, at birth, babies have some 100–200 billion brain cells in place, while you feel like this whole experience has left you with fewer than ten.

•

314. Being a mom means never traveling anywhere without at least five diapers and an extra shirt for yourself. Your husband will understand this only after the baby spits up on his suit.

•

315. Being a mom means suddenly realizing you have that mysterious capability called mother's intuition.

316. Being a mom means
dressing your baby to the nines.

•

317. Being a mom means knowing a
crying baby always wants something—
but not necessarily the same
thing she wanted an hour ago.

•

318. Being a mom means
suddenly realizing how much
noise baby toys make. And that
this is as quiet as childhood gets.

319. Being a mom means knowing
that mother's milk, formula,
and the milk in your refrigerator
all have a place in a child's life.

•

320. Being a mom means dealing
with a child who somehow just
ate diaper cream and Vaseline and
now regrets his menu selection.

•

321. Being a mom means secretly hating
mothers who bring their sick children
over to visit. You know you'll soon
be dodging projectile vomiting.

322. Being a mom means realizing that feeding a baby requires the same organizational skills necessary to feed an army.

•

323. Being a mom means being accused by your husband of spending too much money on baby things. Men are weird that way.

•

324. Being a mom means reading your novels aloud to your baby because you know you need to read them something.

325. Being a mom means
having the pediatrician's
number on speed dial.

•

326. Being a mom means
finding your car keys in your
baby's walker after a frantic
thirty-minute search—and
the perpetrator smiling at you.

•

327. Being a mom means
crying during your
baby's first haircut.

Toddler Moms

328. Being a mom means
learning the "terrible twos" is
false advertising. The condition
lasts longer than a couple of years.

•

329. Being a mom means questioning
your existence, especially during those
times when it's a hot summer day and
your kids are screaming uncontrollable
bloody chaos in their car seats,
and the air conditioner is broken.

•

330. Being a mom means
crawling around on your hands
and knees to get your toddler's
perspective of what she can grab
off tables and stick in her mouth.

331. Being a mom means worrying that if your toddler misses a two-year-old's birthday party, her social development might be affected for life.

•

332. Being a mom means discovering your child is drinking out of the dog's water bowl.

•

333. Being a mom means being the only one who can decipher what your eighteen-month-old means when he says, "Lwiearngsadapiehgthaiej."

334. Being a mom means deciding this whole "balanced life" thing is a myth.

•

335. Being a mom means hearing three words so much, you hear them in your sleep: "Help me, Mommy."

•

336. Being a mom means explaining to a two-year-old why people don't swing on chandeliers.

•

337. Being a mom means advertising in a chat room for a playmate for your little one.

338. Being a mom means suddenly noticing that your child has spent two hours drawing on herself with permanent markers.

•

339. Being a mom means realizing your two-year-old wasn't spreading brown finger paint on the walls. To begin with, you don't have brown finger paint. And, two, her diaper is off.

•

340. Being a mom means having a three-year-old's social life dictate yours.

341. Being a mom means not being able to be alone in the bathroom.

•

342. Being a mom means asking your child what he intends to do with the nose booger between his fingers.

•

343. Being a mom means looking in a whole new way at billboards with half-naked girls.

•

344. Being a mom means explaining to a skeptical only child how much more fun life will be with a new baby in the house.

345. Being a mom means
saying, "Don't hit your brother,"
about ten times a day.

•

346. Being a mom means feeling
guilty if you don't take your child
to Gymboree even though you'd
rather stick needles in your eye.

•

347. Being a mom means sitting
in your closet for hours while your
baby happily plays with your shoes.

•

348. Being a mom means
listening to your child cry
for Daddy instead of for you.

349. Being a mom means not using the words you feel like using because you have a two-year-old listening to every word you say.

•

350. Being a mom means filling out Yale Law School-thick nursery school applications. Perfectly.

•

351. Being a mom means teaching your child to whisper.

•

352. Being a mom means buying goody bags for kids who attend your child's birthday. Dads do not understand this.

353. Being a mom means getting upset because your five-year-old is mistaken for a three-year-old. It doesn't matter that it happens all the time to five-year-olds.

•

354. Being a mom means installing childproof safety latches that you can never open, but that your toddler can open in two seconds.

•

355. Being a mom means measuring your child every three months and announcing how fast she's growing.

356. Being a mom means casually asking how many Ivy League graduates attended the preschool you're thinking about sending your child to.

•

357. Being a mom means teaching a three-year-old to share.

•

358. Being a mom means crying after you drop your child off for the first day of preschool—and then joyfully racing over to the manicurist to get your nails done for the first time in several years.

359. Being a mom means building Lego castles all afternoon. And knowing exactly how many yellow ones, green ones, red ones, and blue ones there are.

•

360. Being a mom means making Mickey Mouse pancakes.

•

361. Being a mom means driving the Mom Car. That's the car that Dad refuses to ride in, with car seats, McDonald's wrappers, diapers sticking out of the glove box, half-empty juice boxes, and a disturbing grape smell.

362. Being a mom means being whacked in the back by a little plastic sword and not knowing whether to laugh, cry, whack back, or tell Dad.

•

363. Being a mom means realizing that the hardest part about not returning to work often has nothing to do with finances.

•

364. Being a mom means you plan on a big night with your husband— only to fall asleep at 8:00 p.m.

•

365. Being a mom means finding a three-foot-tall human appendage clinging to your leg.

366. Being a mom means
looking for restaurants with
quick service because your child
can only sit still for fifteen minutes.

•

367. Being a mom means letting a
three-year-old sculpt the cookie dough.

•

368. Being a mom means seeing
a need for a preschool yearbook.

•

369. Being a mom means planning
to plant flowers, but instead
spending all afternoon watching
your kids dig holes in the garden
and fill them up with water.

370. Being a mom means dancing in the kitchen with a three-year-old.

•

371. Being a mom means putting your child into a playgroup even though you don't know one person.

•

372. Being a mom means searching for a pediatric dentist even though your husband complains it's not worth the cost since all your baby's teeth are going to fall out anyway.

•

373. Being a mom means assuring your child that the tooth fairy will still come even though no one can find the tooth.

374. Being a mom means
worrying about safety every time
your child goes to a playground.

•

375. Being a mom means trying on new
clothes while your child clings to your leg.

•

376. Being a mom means searching
all day for the right sandbox to buy.

•

377. Being a mom means
letting your child do it.

•

378. Being a mom means carrying
a coloring book in your purse.

379. Being a mom means
having a new appreciation for
plastic glasses, bowls, and plates.

•

380. Being a mom means letting
a four-year-old eat a messy
hamburger while sitting on your lap.

•

381. Being a mom means buying
a child-sized table and chairs so you
can have a tea party every afternoon.

•

382. Being a mom means
worrying your child is swallowing the
toothpaste rather than spitting it out.

383. Being a mom means
letting your child brush your teeth
first so you can then brush hers.

•

384. Being a mom means
worrying you're not as sexy as
you were before you had a baby.

•

385. Being a mom means
packing picture books, small toys,
and Cheerios to take to church.

•

386. Being a mom means taking
your child's shoes off during worship
service in order to keep him quiet.

387. Being a mom means apologizing to another mom for your child hitting hers.

•

388. Being a mom means finding your toddler snacking on dog food.

•

389. Being a mom means holding on to a child who is doing the spaghetti wriggle.

•

390. Being a mom means you're in charge of the mittens, shoes, gloves, and bathing suits—and these are always missing.

•

391. Being a mom means packing fifty toys into a beach bag just to go to the swimming pool for two hours.

392. Being a mom means packing special goodies when traveling to keep everyone fed, busy, distracted, and quiet.

•

393. Being a mom means getting begged for chocolate milk. For eighteen years.

•

394. Being a mom means learning thirty different games to play at your child's four-year-old birthday party.

•

395. Being a mom means teaching children that their needs do not automatically outweigh others'.

396. Being a mom means taking your kids to the pool because they need sun—and then slapping three layers of 50-SPF sunblock on them.

•

397. Being a mom means trying to play in the pool with your kids without getting your hair wet.

•

398. Being a mom means buying your kids chewable vitamins. Even when they're in high school.

•

399. Being a mom means knowing the names of all the local magicians who do kiddy parties.

400. Being a mom means teaching the words *please* and *thank you*.

•

401. Being a mom means recognizing when a misbehaving child is simply tired and hungry.

•

402. Being a mom means sitting in the baby pool holding a pail while your child stands at the side of the pool and cries.

•

403. Being a mom means giving your kids a hose and a sprinkler and telling them to have fun.

404. Being a mom means taking kids to the library for story time.

●

405. Being a mom means coloring Easter eggs and buying everyone an Easter basket. Even though the only thing your kids care about is the candy.

●

406. Being a mom means letting your kids feel the sense of accomplishment that comes with dressing themselves, even if they put on yellow shorts, cowboy boots, swim goggles, and a cape.

●

407. Being a mom means depending on a baggie of Cheerios to calm down your cranky kid.

408. Being a mom means developing your own parenting style. In the face of helpful advice from your parents, friends, in-laws, brothers, and sisters.

•

409. Being a mom means taking your kids to the playground so they can run free—and then panicking when you lose sight of them.

•

410. Being a mom means pushing swings for an hour because you're hopelessly addicted to the sounds of your children's laughter.

411. Being a mom means making
your children feel brave by acting
as if you're afraid they'll get hurt
when you know they're perfectly safe.

•

412. Being a mom means feeling
bewildered when your five-year-old
says he doesn't want to go to the
bathroom with you anymore because
he wants to use the men's room.

•

413. Being a mom means smiling
and saying, "It looks really good,"
after your four-year-old has just cut
off her hair with the kitchen scissors.

414. Being a mom means proudly displaying the clay thing your child made in kindergarten.

•

415. Being a mom means eating chocolate-chip cookies with your kids even though you're on a diet.

•

416. Being a mom means teaching your children that throwing a tantrum will lead to misery, not to getting their way.

•

417. Being a mom means buying concert tickets for Raffi when you really want to go to the U2 concert.

418. Being a mom means listening to your toddler announce that her brother just ate a worm.

•

419. Being a mom means developing a deep love for Velcro.

•

420. Being a mom means trying to fit three car seats in a backseat that was meant to handle two.

•

421. Being a mom means covering your child's eyes in a theater.

•

422. Being a mom means making sure breakfast gets eaten every morning. Even if it comes out of a cereal box.

423. Being a mom means being the judge.

•

424. Being a mom means quizzing potential baby-sitters with questions like: "What would you do if my kids refused to do what you say?"; "What would you do if they were running a fever?"; and "What would you do if they threatened to hold their breath until they passed out?"

•

425. Being a mom means withholding the name of your favorite baby-sitter from your best friend.

426. Being a mom means understanding that love and patience are much better character traits than perfection.

•

427. Being a mom means looking forward to your child's naps because it means you can take one.

•

428. Being a mom means getting a traffic ticket while your child screams in the backseat of the car.

•

429. Being a mom means buying a certain cereal because there are toys inside the box.

430. Being a mom means spending an hour looking all over the house for mittens, gloves, parkas, and scarves, so your kids can spend ten minutes outside in the snow.

•

431. Being a mom means teaching and reinforcing core values in a society that doesn't seem to have any.

•

432. Being a mom means packing food and drinks for a car trip even though the whole family wants to stop somewhere and eat.

433. Being a mom means worrying whether the vacation hotel is nice enough—and then realizing the only thing the kids care about is the swimming pool. A vibrating bed is cool too.

•

434. Being a mom means having all the answers.

•

435. Being a mom means holding wriggly kids in place at the Target portrait studio.

•

436. Being a mom means announcing to your kids that their eyes will become stuck if they keep crossing them.

437. Being a mom means knowing a child's moral development is dependent on his emotional well-being.

•

438. Being a mom means wondering if you should do anything about your children standing naked in the backyard playing with the hose and deciding that, since they're being quiet, you'll leave the whole thing alone.

•

439. Being a mom means crying in the parking lot because your twenty-five-pound child refuses to get in the car seat.

440. Being a mom means limiting your friends to only those people who agree your children rank just below the second coming.

•

441. Being a mom means hiding *The Lion King* because you've seen it a thousand times.

•

442. Being a mom means wiping runny noses with your sleeve.

•

443. Being a mom means kissing a dirty, sticky, smelly face when you'd rather not.

444. Being a mom means
reassuring your husband that
everything will work out fine.

•

445. Being a mom means realizing you're
not the most effective disciplinarian in
the family. Your heart is too soft.

•

446. Being a mom means catching
something from your child that
gave them a fever for four hours,
but lays you flat for four days.

•

447. Being a mom means
finding your daughter playing
with the expensive makeup
you saved two months to buy.

448. Being a mom means finding your child holding a garden hose in the game room. With the water on.

•

449. Being a mom means breaking down in tears in the car after you drop your child off at day care for the first time.

•

450. Being a mom means offering your child (read "bribing with") a cookie to sit on the toilet. Well, a lot of cookies.

•

451. Being a mom means realizing great teenagers are created in childhood.

452. Being a mom means
using the TV to entertain your
kids while you make dinner—
and then feeling guilty about it.

•

**453. Being a mom means finding ways
to agree with your child's father on how
to approach child raising. Whether
you're still married to him or not.**

•

454. Being a mom means wondering
if your three-year-old's temper
tantrums mean that she has Tourette's.

455. Being a mom means somehow teaching your kids to never talk to strangers unless they're lost because then strangers are okay. (If you're confused, imagine how confused your kids are.)

•

456. Being a mom means teaching your kids to scream, break things, bite, kick, or do whatever they need to do to get away from a dangerous situation.

•

457. Being a mom means teaching kids their name, both their parents' names, their address, and their phone number. And constantly testing them on this vital information.

458. Being a mom means teaching kids that if they're approached by a stranger driving a car, to run in the opposite direction and tell an adult they know what just happened.

•

459. Being a mom means telling kids that if they're forced into a stranger's car, to jump into the stranger's lap, honk the horn, and try to press on the gas to cause an accident.

•

460. Being a mom means talking about strangers, predators, and the tricks they use.

461. Being a mom means practicing "what if" situations at home. Ask: "What if you're lost at the mall?"; "What if someone frightens you?"; and "What if a stranger says, 'Your mom sent me to pick you up'?"

•

462. Being a mom means driving kids to karate three times a week so they'll know how to defend themselves.

•

463. Being a mom means becoming an expert on contagious diseases.

464. Being a mom means agreeing to guinea pigs, rabbits, turtles, goldfish, hamsters, and birds in an effort to avoid a dog.

•

465. Being a mom means finding the turtle—alive—in the washing machine. While unloading the clean clothes.

•

466. Being a mom means taking a child to the dog shelter to just "look" at the dogs knowing the risk involved.

•

467. Being a mom means listening to the Wiggles when you'd rather listen to Gwen Stefani.

468. Being a mom means giving your seven-year-old your undivided attention while she tells you—in excruciating detail—all about her day.

•

469. Being a mom means getting begged to go to the toy store.

•

470. Being a mom means buying a pretend toaster that's as expensive as the real thing.

•

471. Being a mom means going to parades when you'd rather go back to bed.

472. Being a mom means reading the same book over and over and over and over and over again because your child loves it.

•

473. Being a mom means telling your kids what they're going to do, not asking them if they'd "like" to do something. This makes raising teenagers a lot easier.

•

474. Being a mom means wondering if delaying your child's entrance into kindergarten would help him gain admittance into Harvard.

475. Being a mom means
going to bed in tears because
you screamed at your child who
screamed at you for two hours.

•

476. Being a mom means meaning
what you say. Your child will start
testing this at nine months—and
continue until she leaves home.

•

477. Being a mom means giving up
on the idea of a *House Beautiful*
home and moving all glass, crystal,
china, and statuettes to places
two-year-old hands can't reach.

478. Being a mom means having a designated throw-up bowl and yanking it out anytime one of your kids looks pale.

•

479. Being a mom means knowing more than you think you know.

•

480. Being a mom means listening to everything your five-year-old has to say about her day.

•

481. Being a mom means craving time alone.

482. Being a mom means
making the rules.

•

483. Being a mom means knowing that
if a kid is barfing near your kid, you
yourself will probably be barfing soon.

•

484. Being a mom means
teaching a little girl that throwing
food is as much fun as eating it.

•

485. Being a mom means
picking your son's nose for him.

•

486. Being a mom means
laughing at really dumb jokes.

487. Being a mom means thinking the best afternoon in the world is curling up with a four-year-old and watching *Shrek* for the two hundredth time.

•

488. Being a mom means having to apologize to the tiniest members of the family for your humanness.

•

489. Being a mom means teaching your kids to read before they start kindergarten.

•

490. Being a mom means actually eating a putty dough cake so your daughter won't get her feelings hurt.

491. Being a mom means having a toddler throw a temper tantrum in the mall and assuming everyone is judging you when they're actually feeling sorry for you.

•

492. Being a mom means thinking a French cooking class for five-year-olds makes sense. Then realizing you were temporarily insane.

•

493. Being a mom means wondering how the whole family could have clean laundry except for you.

494. Being a mom means carrying a children's book in your purse to read whenever the two of you are stuck in a waiting room.

•

495. Being a mom means not forgetting the bread when you go see the ducks. Or—if you forget— stopping at McDonald's, buying a children's burger, throwing away the meat, and then heading to the park.

•

496. Being a mom means being your child's best teacher.

497. Being a mom means knowing your house is a lot messier than those in magazine ads. And being okay with it.

•

498. Being a mom means realizing everything you do now will impact the sixteen-year-old your child becomes.

•

499. Being a mom means never believing for one second your child is average.

•

500. Being a mom means catching the Asian flu in the pediatrician's office.

501. Being a mom means hiring
Spiderman for a birthday party.

•

502. Being a mom means buying a
$100 frame for your child's finger-paint
artwork and hanging it in the living room.

•

503. Being a mom means
making a rainy day fun.

•

504. Being a mom means pulling your
kids around the block in a wagon.

•

505. Being a mom means lying down
with a sick child. Knowing the risks.

506. Being a mom means hating
the moms in magazines who seem to
have perfect children, perfect bodies,
perfect husbands, perfect nannies,
and a perfectly wonderful time.

•

507. Being a mom means
giving a pancake a happy face with
whipped cream and chocolate chips.

•

508. Being a mom means taking
your kids to a pumpkin patch.
And bringing home a pumpkin
you can't lift out of your car.

•

509. Being a mom means sending your
nanny or baby-sitter to a CPR class.

510. Being a mom means
kissing little noses.

•

511. Being a mom means fitting a
child's minikitchen into your kitchen.

•

512. Being a mom means being
overwhelmingly busy or stiflingly
bored. Often in the same day.

•

513. Being a mom means
biting your child's nail when
you can't find the nail clippers.

•

514. Being a mom means trying to explain
death and then reassuring your kids
that there's no reason to be afraid.

515. Being a mom means having a garage sale to get rid of your old stuff so you can make room for your child's new stuff.

•

516. Being a mom means treating a skinned knee with a kiss.

•

517. Being a mom means having your children love to smell you.

•

518. Being a mom means saying, "You're going to get in trouble when your father gets home," because you know even the most belligerent child doesn't want to deal with an angry dad.

Moms of
School Kids

519. Being a mom means inexplicably breaking down in tears when your child starts first grade just like you did when she started preschool. Husbands will not understand this.

•

520. Being a mom means worrying everyone in school is bigger than your child.

•

521. Being a mom means memorizing the school locker combination because somebody in the family needs to know it.

522. Being a mom means
enforcing a family reading time.

•

523. Being a mom means
telling them story after story
about you when you were their age.

•

524. Being a mom means walking kids
to the school bus even when they tell
you they're old enough to go alone.

•

525. Being a mom means having
your child ask you about sex
when you're standing in an
elevator with a group of strangers.

526. Being a mom means embarrassing your kids by taking back-to-school pictures in front of their friends.

•

527. Being a mom means giving up the cool convertible for a minivan.

•

528. Being a mom means enrolling your child in Vacation Bible School.

•

529. Being a mom means volunteering to drive a carload of kids to the science museum and finding it closed. Then immediately coming up with a Plan B. Like Chuck E. Cheese.

530. Being a mom means being
the only one in the family to
believe combed hair is important.

•

531. Being a mom means
reminding your kids that,
yes, you are the boss of them.

•

532. Being a mom means finding
all your spoons bent backward
from kids trying to scoop ice cream.

•

533. Being a mom means
getting begged to watch TV.

534. Being a mom means
helping your third-grader write
three sentences about Honduras.

•

535. Being a mom means
believing your children are
hearing impaired since they
don't seem to hear a thing you say.

•

536. Being a mom means
stressing over your first-grader's
sadness when another first-
grader won't be her best friend.

537. Being a mom means worrying about the message it will send if you get your ten-year-old a cell phone—then getting one anyway because you're worried about his safety. Then, once again, worrying about the message it will send. Then deciding your eight-year-old also needs one.

•

538. Being a mom means telling your child to not pick their nose—then seeing something in there and going after it.

539. Being a mom means
smelling your children to
make sure they really did bathe.

•

540. Being a mom means keeping
a family calendar. Maybe two.

•

541. Being a mom means
taking everyone to the library
every few weeks for new books.

•

542. Being a mom means counting
the days till school starts.

543. Being a mom means
searching through backpacks
for notes from the teacher.

•

544. Being a mom means serving
cinnamon rolls every morning
because you don't care what your kids
eat as long as they actually do eat.

•

545. Being a mom means standing on
the sidelines cheering for your child
even though you don't have the faintest
concept of the rules of the game.

546. Being a mom means planning your vacation around a hotel that advertises the "largest pool slide in the state."

•

547. Being a mom means sneaking spinach into grilled-cheese sandwiches.

•

548. Being a mom means being grateful your kids can take care of themselves and watch TV when you are too sick to move.

549. Being a mom means knowing what is being served in the school cafeteria because you have the monthly menu on your refrigerator.

•

550. Being a mom means trying to convince your kids they don't hate school.

•

551. Being a mom means scanning all your kids' artwork onto a DVD.

•

552. Being a mom means hoping and praying your child doesn't ask you what that Viagra commercial was all about.

553. Being a mom means telling your son how big his muscles are while his dad is telling him his arms are puny.

•

554. Being a mom means realizing your daughter just had a lunch of potato chips dipped in ketchup.

•

555. Being a mom means talking about AIDS. At dinner. Even though the whole family wants to talk about something else.

•

556. Being a mom means realizing when kids get hungry enough, they'll eat spinach.

557. Being a mom means getting begged for a video game system.

•

558. Being a mom means stressing the importance of education.

•

559. Being a mom means spending your best years in a car driving to tennis lessons, gymnastic lessons, French lessons, piano lessons, and swimming lessons, not to mention school, field trips, stores, and playdates.

•

560. Being a mom means freaking out if you think your child has a learning disability. Then learning it's manageable.

561. Being a mom means setting a routine. Your kids may joke about it, but they'll depend on it.

•

562. Being a mom means reading to an eleven-year-old because he still loves when you do.

•

563. Being a mom means teaching your child's Sunday-school class.

•

564. Being a mom means taking time to be alone with each child.

565. Being a mom means
volunteering to be team mom.

•

566. Being a mom means
teaching your child to be kind.

•

567. Being a mom means knowing your
kids will come home from school hungry,
exhausted, and mentally scattered.

•

568. Being a mom means finding
thirteen old lunch sacks under
the kids' beds. And realizing
that's where all those Rubbermaid
containers went. And that smell...

569. Being a mom means feeling that other moms throw better birthday parties, make better Valentine's Day gifts, and pack more exciting lunches— and then realizing your kids don't care.

•

570. Being a mom means working on a diorama at 1:00 a.m. for a school science-fair project while everyone else in the house sleeps.

•

571. Being a mom means buying each of your kids a Valentine's Day card every year, even after they've left for college.

572. Being a mom means volunteering to bring something for the bake sale— and then running to the store to buy a cake because you've run out of time.

•

573. Being a mom means teaching your kids not to change who they are in order to please someone else.

•

574. Being a mom means talking to teachers about what books kids are reading for fun—and then buying them.

•

575. Being a mom means finding your child's list of spelling words for the week in the laundry.

576. Being a mom means
using each of the spelling words
in sentences. All week long.

•

577. Being a mom means
remembering that your most
important relationship is with God.

•

578. Being a mom means telling your
kids soft drinks are bad for them—
yet buying soft drinks by the case.

•

579. Being a mom means hiding candy
bars in the back of your closet and
eating them after the kids go to bed.

580. Being a mom means putting "I love you" notes in lunch boxes.

•

581. Being a mom means turning off the TV because you want the family to discuss their day— and having nobody say anything.

•

582. Being a mom means forgetting excellence should be expected and only occasionally rewarded.

•

583. Being a mom means being able to find your way around the mall blindfolded.

584. Being a mom means reading all the mom blogs to see if you've given birth to a space alien or if all your experiences are normal.

•

585. Being a mom means not even considering that you worry more than you should.

•

586. Being a mom means having a twelve-year-old on whom you've spent the equivalent of the domestic GNP, who now doesn't want to be seen with you at the movies.

587. Being a mom means raising your
kids to be able to live without you.

•

588. Being a mom means putting the
kids to bed early because you want
to spend time with your husband.
Who then says he's going running.

•

589. Being a mom means leaving the mall
with a car full of kids and being told five
minutes later that one of them is missing.

•

590. Being a mom means getting
begged to allow a sleepover.

591. Being a mom means
worrying the teachers like
the other kids more than yours.

•

592. Being a mom means
praising your child. A lot.

•

593. Being a mom means
taking the teacher's side.

•

594. Being a mom means
working all afternoon to make a
PTA dinner for the teachers—only
to learn it gave them food poisoning.

595. Being a mom means
wondering late at night if
motherhood really is the most
meaningful experience in your life.

•

596. Being a mom means
telling the teacher you just want
your child to be treated fairly
when what you really want
is special consideration.

•

597. Being a mom means
embarrassing your kids—
without meaning or trying to.

598. Being a mom means you can go to the circus without having to borrow children.

•

599. Being a mom means discovering a latent compulsion to bake.

•

600. Being a mom means starting every adult conversation with "How are your kids?" because, curiously, all your friends are your children's friends' parents.

•

601. Being a mom means sticking your nose in your child's throat to smell their breath.

602. Being a mom means buying mouthwash and toothpaste for your child hoping that, by some miracle, those items will be used.

•

603. Being a mom means getting sick with worry and stress over your child's soccer, ballet, baseball, and singing tryouts. Your child, of course, is fine.

•

604. Being a mom means actually believing other parents get their kids to do homework without a fight.

605. Being a mom means
wondering if the founder of
Chuck E. Cheese can live with himself.

•

606. Being a mom means agreeing to
coach a soccer team so your daughter can
be on a team. Even if you've never played.

•

607. Being a mom means joining the PTA,
immediately becoming a committee chair,
then wondering how you became so busy.

•

608. Being a mom means
setting the parental controls
on video games and the Internet.

609. Being a mom means
spending Saturdays on a soccer
field instead of at a spa salon.

•

610. Being a mom means volunteering at
school so you can keep an eye on things.

•

611. Being a mom means making
a nutritious lunch every morning that
your son trades at noon for doughnuts.

•

612. Being a mom means going to bed at
night worrying if your child is happy.

•

613. Being a mom means being able to
make sense of the carpool lane at school.

614. Being a mom means gazing at the moon with your kids even though it's past their bedtime.

•

615. Being a mom means searching all over town for the right soccer cleats even though they all look the same to you.

•

616. Being a mom means smelling your child's lunch box and wondering if something died in there.

•

617. Being a mom means scheduling every hour of your child's life because you're afraid if you don't, another child will get ahead.

618. Being a mom means spying on your kids when you take them to the mall.

•

619. Being a mom means finding notes from other kids in backpacks and in pockets. And reading them.

•

620. Being a mom means arranging your work hours so you can be home when your kids come home from school.

•

621. Being a mom means bonding with your child in the kitchen.

622. Being a mom means
spending all afternoon in
the car. Every afternoon.

•

623. Being a mom means
recognizing the cosmetic industry
sees you as a prospect, but your
daughters as the source of real dough.

•

624. Being a mom means
finding homework in backpacks
that was never turned in.

625. Being a mom means having your child read a menu out loud.

•

626. Being a mom means wearing a really ugly T-shirt that announces, "I'm Kelly's mom!"

•

627. Being a mom means worrying the older kids will be mean to yours.

•

628. Being a mom means cooking okra even though you know everybody hates it, but they need something green in their life.

629. Being a mom means eating the okra to prove how good it tastes—and then gagging.

•

630. Being a mom means knowing the first names of the doctors in the ER.

•

631. Being a mom means telling your kids every move they make on the Internet will be monitored by you. And doing so.

632. Being a mom means
worrying about your
kids' mean friends.

•

633. Being a mom means
wanting to call the mothers
of those kids who are being mean
to yours, but you know you can't.

•

634. Being a mom means
freaking out when you learn
your kids' friends are
becoming sexually active.

635. Being a mom means
asking your kids what
sex means to them.

•

636. Being a mom means
knowing middle school is
its own particular kind of hell.

•

637. Being a mom means teaching that
french fries don't qualify as vegetables
and donuts don't count as grain.

Moms and Computers

638. Being a mom means having children beg for a computer, beg to put the computer in their room, and beg to let them join MySpace.

•

639. Being a mom means vowing your child will never belong to MySpace—then being talked into it.

•

640. Being a mom means explaining the importance of never revealing to anyone private information like your address, phone number, social security number, screen names, or credit card numbers.

641. Being a mom means teaching your kids to never post on the Internet where they hang out every day after school.

•

642. Being a mom means keeping the computer in the den where everybody can see what's going on.

•

643. Being a mom means explaining there are creeps on the Internet who are not who they say they are.

644. Being a mom means teaching kids that downloading off the Internet movies or songs that they haven't paid for is, well, stealing.

•

645. Being a mom means deciding a teen blog is a good thing if it means your kids will start writing every day.

•

646. Being a mom means reminding kids anything they say or post on the Internet today can be held against them three or four years later.

647. Being a mom means teaching kids how to block unwanted messages from unwanted people.

•

648. Being a mom means letting your teenager talk you into setting up a MySpace page for yourself and praying none of your friends find out about it.

649. Being a mom means reading your child's MySpace page daily, because that's how you really learn what's going on.

•

650. Being a mom means asking your twelve-year-old for help downloading a file.

Moms of Teens

651. Being a mom means wondering why your teen has nothing to say when you ask how their day went.

•

652. Being a mom means hearing other adults comment about how your teen is a great conversationalist.

•

653. Being a mom means knowing where your kids are.

•

654. Being a mom means being told, "I'm too old for this!" And knowing they're still too young.

655. Being a mom means
wanting to tell your kids how
to fix every problem in their life,
but all they want you to do is listen.

•

656. Being a mom means getting upset
when a coach yells at your child.

•

657. Being a mom means
feeling your children's pain
when they get benched or don't
get the part or lose their position.

658. Being a mom means giving your children a diary and telling them to fill it in. They can write anything they like, they don't have to worry about punctuation, and they can write down their feelings without being criticized.

•

659. Being a mom means suffering more than your kids do in middle school because you know you can't make everything all right.

•

660. Being a mom means deciding which TV shows and movies are too violent.

661. Being a mom means
trying to like your kids' music.

•

662. Being a mom means knowing
your kids are too stubborn to ask
for help, so you barge in and start
helping. And they don't appreciate it.

•

663. Being a mom means
relearning algebra.

•

664. Being a mom means
reminding your kids to use
"please" and "thank you."

665. Being a mom means always knowing your child's reading level.

•

666. Being a mom means having your kids ask you for money because they know better than to ask their dad.

•

667. Being a mom means checking your kids out of school on a cool spring day and playing eighteen holes.

•

668. Being a mom means not dressing like you're eighteen.

669. Being a mom means listening without commenting. It's an acquired skill. That could take a lifetime to learn.

•

670. Being a mom means thinking about what you're going to say before you say it. Maybe thinking about it two or three times.

•

671. Being a mom means wearing a button with your child's face on it at games and performances.

672. Being a mom means
buying acne medicine.

•

673. Being a mom means talking
about college even though your
daughter wants to talk about
what movie stars are wearing.

•

674. Being a mom means
being the fashion police.

•

675. Being a mom means, at times,
confiscating your child's computer,
cell phone, iPod, and DVD player.

676. Being a mom means having the courage to be uncool, especially when it comes to curfews, parties, and fashions.

•

677. Being a mom means learning that your teenager hasn't read a book since the semester started— and that exams start in two days.

•

678. Being a mom means telling your children how important to you they are.

•

679. Being a mom means saying, "You're not going to school looking like that."

680. Being a mom means worrying your child is falling behind in class.

•

681. Being a mom means realizing that sometimes the only way to get a teenager talking is for you to start talking.

•

682. Being a mom means knowing your kids don't need you to be another friend. They need a mom.

683. Being a mom means believing "Because I said so!" is a perfectly rational answer to the question "Why?"

684. Being a mom means knowing your kids don't want to be seen with you and taking them shopping at the mall anyway.

•

685. Being a mom means being furious that the PTA, which you never wanted to join, didn't elect you vice president.

•

686. Being a mom means telling your daughter at breakfast that her top is too low, her skirt is too high, and she'd better put on something that makes her look like a nerd. Now.

687. Being a mom means putting "Don't Touch" labels in the refrigerator.

•

688. Being a mom means charging your child's friends for the bread, the potato chips, and the fruit juice they consume every day at your house.

•

689. Being a mom means wanting to follow your daughter on her first car date. And being upset when your husband isn't as worried as you are.

690. Being a mom means sucking up to the teacher who's about to fail your kid.

•

691. Being a mom means worrying about whether your teenager is in the right clique.

•

692. Being a mom means sitting in the stands in pouring rain with a 101° fever, so your child can see you watching her when she plays.

•

693. Being a mom means knowing your kids love you even though they're too embarrassed to say so.

694. Being a mom means
insisting your kids buy clothes
you pick out because you think
you know what's fashionable.

•

695. Being a mom means working up the
courage to talk to your kids about sex.

•

696. Being a mom means
worrying your kids know
more about sex than you do.

•

697. Being a mom means
explaining to obstinate teenagers
how fun the family vacation will be.

698. Being a mom means calling other parents to make sure they'll be home when your teenager is invited to a party at their house.

•

699. Being a mom means rubbing your seventeen-year-old's back at the end of the day even though you can barely lift your arms.

•

700. Being a mom means having the right medicine available for any emergency. If only you can find it.

•

701. Being a mom means being able to relax only when everyone is in bed.

702. Being a mom means
every now and then having
your teenager read out loud.

•

703. Being a mom means
hiring a tutor because no one in
your family understands calculus.

•

704. Being a mom means
worrying your teen isn't building
an impressive résumé, even though
she's only fourteen years old.

705. Being a mom means learning teen-speak like "bf," "d8," "p911," and "pal."

•

706. Being a mom means realizing your daughter is totally different from you. And, over time, accepting it.

•

707. Being a mom means deciding you don't need to explain things. You just want your way.

708. Being a mom means
asking every now and then,
"What's the most important thing in
your life right now?" and marveling
because you didn't know your
children would answer that way.

•

709. Being a mom means
telling your teenager to get a job
because you can't afford his lifestyle.

•

710. Being a mom means hoping to
prevent your kids from experiencing
the pain of life. And failing.

711. Being a mom means
having a broken heart whenever
your child's heart is broken.

•

712. Being a mom means saying,
"Grades aren't that important"—
then making an appointment with
the teacher because your child
didn't come home with an A.

•

713. Being a mom means accepting
your child is making life more difficult
than it has to be. And letting them.

•

714. Being a mom means
being their biggest fan.

715. Being a mom means nagging
your children to fill out college
applications during their junior year.

•

716. Being a mom means making them a
scrapbook of all their teenage pictures.

•

717. Being a mom means
forcing yourself to stay awake at
11:30 p.m. because that's when
your high schooler wants to talk.

•

718. Being a mom means taking
a college road trip with your
high school senior and realizing
how much you'll miss this person.

719. Being a mom means thinking,
at 10:00 p.m. Friday night,
that your teenager—not you—
should be working on his college
applications instead of partying.

•

720. Being a mom means
telling everyone, even the cashier
at the dry cleaners, which colleges
have sent acceptance letters.

•

721. Being a mom means
taking your kids to college
to help them "settle in."

722. Being a mom means decorating their dorm while they're out all day meeting people on campus.

•

723. Being a mom means standing in line with them at registration and asking parents around you what they know about the professors listed in the course guide.

•

724. Being a mom means crying when you leave your child at college. And remembering you felt the same way their first day of preschool.

Moms of
Adult Kids

725. Being a mom means asking your twenty-two-year-old, in front of his date, about his constipation issues.

•

726. Being a mom means realizing your daughter's purse is more expensive than yours. And she's still in college.

•

727. Being a mom is thinking you have to make all the decisions for your kids, even though they're twenty-five.

•

728. Being a mom means forgetting that your child's professors don't want to hear from you.

729. Being a mom means remembering all the weekends you spent at your kids' games. And not missing them.

•

730. Being a mom means remembering all the close relationships you had with your kids' friends' parents, but never seeing those people again after the high school graduation.

•

731. Being a mom means loving your child's significant other.

•

732. Being a mom means crying when your child breaks up with that person.

733. Being a mom means giving advice when you know you shouldn't, but you can't help it.

•

734. Being a mom means serving as a career counselor.

•

735. Being a mom means showing up for your child's on-campus interviews.

•

736. Being a mom means writing and polishing their résumé.

•

737. Being a mom means wondering how anybody looking the way your child looks could ever get hired—anywhere.

738. Being a mom means calling
the company that didn't hire
your child and finding out why.

•

739. Being a mom means insisting
your child learn three different
routes to his job interview in case
there's a wreck stopping traffic.

•

740. Being a mom means
telling your child to be sure
to sign up for the insurance.

•

741. Being a mom means thinking—
just momentarily—about calling
your child's prospective employer
to negotiate the salary.

742. Being a mom means displaying graduation pictures in your living room, your bedroom, your desk, and your office.

•

743. Being a mom means calling the boss of your twenty-five-year-old daughter and asking how she's doing at work. And not seeing anything wrong with that.

•

744. Being a mom means buying wedding presents for kids you hardly know because you plan to send their parents a wedding invitation someday.

745. Being a mom means telling the president of your son's company that your son shouldn't have to work over a holiday.

•

746. Being a mom means renting a beach house instead of a hotel room so "all the kids can come."

•

747. Being a mom means getting a phone call from an upset child, becoming alarmed, doing your best to make them feel better, hearing a call-waiting "beep," and then hearing them say, "Gotta go!"

748. Being a mom means
noticing your son needs to
shave. No matter how old he is.

•

749. Being a mom means
buying toilet paper for your adult
kids because you don't think
they'll buy it on their own.

•

750. Being a mom means
waking up your husband late
at night to worry with you over
your child not getting a promotion.

751. Being a mom means worrying about whether your thirty-year-old is lonely, then calling her to come to dinner, and being told she's eating with her friends.

•

752. Being a mom means wondering if your kids will ever get married.

•

753. Being a mom means trying to serve a family dinner to a vegetarian, a meat lover, and someone who's lactose intolerant.

754. Being a mom means buying more food than you need in case your kids show up for dinner.

•

755. Being a mom means sitting on a couch with your twenty-one-year-old and looking at their childhood pictures.

•

756. Being a mom means worrying when your twenty-five-year-old is driving at night in a rainstorm.

757. Being a mom means letting your twenty-four-year-old pick out clothes for you.

•

758. Being a mom means thinking your kids are mad at you if they haven't called you in three days.

•

759. Being a mom means worrying your child only has a bachelor of arts degree when everyone today has a master's.

760. Being a mom means listening to your kids share their favorite childhood memories and having no idea what they're talking about.

•

761. Being a mom means learning that incidents you've completely forgotten are, years later, what the kids remember most.

•

762. Being a mom means coming to grips with the fact your kids can make it on their own.

Working Moms

763. Being a mom means
getting everybody out of
the house by 7:30 a.m.

•

764. Being a mom means learning
what the Mommy Track means.

•

765. Being a mom means
deciding between career and family.
And forever worrying if you chose right.

•

766. Being a mom means
trying to explain the missing
years on your résumé.

767. Being a mom means worrying if you'll still be the most important person in the world to your baby after you go back to work.

•

768. Being a mom means picking a job because of medical benefits.

•

769. Being a mom means deciding nobody in the media ever had a baby.

•

770. Being a mom means going to work with barf all over your blazer. And telling your clients to deal with it.

771. Being a mom means negotiating with your employer for a maternity leave. And getting an unpaid one.

•

772. Being a mom means being up front about family commitments during job interviews.

•

773. Being a mom means turning off your Blackberry when you get home.

•

774. Being a mom means continuing to show pictures of your kids to fellow employees when they'd rather see pictures of your turtle.

775. Being a mom means thinking that every time you take your eyes off your child to do some work, you'll miss a magic moment.

•

776. Being a mom means calling home to make sure everybody's doing homework instead of watching TV.

•

777. Being a mom means finishing your spreadsheet analysis instead of gratefully napping when your children nap. And being ready with milk and cookies when they wake up.

778. Being a mom means making your family your priority whether you work outside the home or not.

•

779. Being a mom means developing your negotiation skills. At home as well as at work.

•

780. Being a mom means turning down a promotion because you would have to travel more.

•

781. Being a mom means realizing you haven't been to the gym in weeks.

782. Being a mom means knowing
the term *working parents* is
code for *working mothers*.

•

783. Being a mom means
you're less likely to be hired.

•

784. Being a mom means you're likely to
earn less than a childless woman earns.

•

785. Being a mom means not being
able to imagine not going back
to work—then not being able
to imagine leaving your baby.

786. Being a mom means leaving your PDA at home when you go on vacation.

•

787. Being a mom means trying to do business over the phone while a child cries in the background.

•

788. Being a mom means the last thing you want to do when you get home at night is discipline your children. So you spend the first hour or so when you get home just visiting with them. You know you'll have to be "mean mom" shortly.

789. Being a mom means choosing schools because of their after-school programs.

•

790. Being a mom means delegating responsibilities to your husband and kids so the household can function.

•

791. Being a mom means getting yourself ready for work before waking up your kids. Totally ready.

•

792. Being a mom means having to leave work so you can take your child the lunch she forgot to grab before leaving for school.

793. Being a mom means sitting at the kitchen table while your child does homework when you really want to be sitting in a hot bath.

•

794. Being a mom means exercising at 6:00 a.m. while your kids are still sleeping.

•

795. Being a mom means not going to bed until you finish packing lunches and backpacks.

796. Being a mom means
getting begged by your kids
not to take them to day care.

•

797. Being a mom means
playing hooky from work
to spend time with your kids.

•

798. Being a mom means
taking time off from work
to volunteer in the classroom.

•

799. Being a mom means trading
e-mails with the teacher on your
Blackberry while you sit in a meeting.

800. Being a mom means
constantly worrying if day
care is good for your child.

•

801. Being a mom means
getting a family up, showered,
clothed, fed, and out of the
house in ninety minutes.

•

802. Being a mom means
having a special appreciation for
meals that are a telephone call away.

803. Being a mom means making sure someone is always there to welcome your kids home, even if that someone isn't you.

•

804. Being a mom means wanting to know the life history of your child-care provider.

•

805. Being a mom means getting upset with your child-care provider over something your four-year-old told you, even though you know your four-year-old isn't the most reliable source of information.

806. Being a mom means
starting a home-based business.

•

807. Being a mom means dropping
in at the day care unannounced.

•

808. Being a mom means
infecting the person who
works next to you with the flu your
child brought home from school.

•

809. Being a mom means getting
down on the floor with your kids
when you first walk in the house
because it's good for both of you.

241

810. Being a mom means staying home with your sick child even though you had three meetings that day.

•

811. Being a mom means telling your boss you have to leave for an important appointment and then taking your child to a birthday party.

•

812. Being a mom means wishing you were listening to your baby's laughter rather than your client's babble.

813. Being a mom means loving
the time alone when you travel.
And feeling guilty about it.

•

814. Being a mom means having
to decide whether to miss work or
send your sick child to day care
because you can't afford the time off.

•

815. Being a mom means
being less than thrilled when
school declares a snow day.

816. Being a mom means planning dinners a week in advance.

•

817. Being a mom means trying to discipline a child over the phone.

•

818. Being a mom means using your Crock-Pot more than your oven.

•

819. Being a mom means making business contacts at your kids' school.

820. Being a mom means
closing a business deal on the
phone while a four-year-old
is asleep on your lap.

•

821. Being a mom means
understanding you can
have it all...just not all at once.

Single Moms

822. Being a single mom means knowing that, while two-parent homes are best for children, life doesn't always work out that way.

•

823. Being a single mom means wrestling with how to put your children first when you're in a new relationship.

•

824. Being a single mom means deciding you don't have the time to make a new relationship work.

825. Being a single mom
means feeling as though
you're living on a treadmill.

•

826. Being a single mom means
sometimes working two jobs.

•

827. Being a single mom means thinking
five hours of sleep is a good night.

•

828. Being a single mom
means discussing things with
your children that married moms
discuss with their husbands.

829. Being a single mom
means having a baby-sitter cancel
an hour before a job interview—
and still getting the job.

•

830. Being a single mom means
worrying more about money than
you ever have before in your life.

•

831. Being a single mom
means accepting any and all
hand-me-downs from friends,
families, even complete strangers.

832. Being a single mom means prospective employers will judge you negatively because you're a single parent.

•

833. Being a single mom means having to answer when your child asks, "Where is Daddy?"

•

834. Being a single mom means paying someone good money to watch your baby for two hours while you take a bath and a nap.

835. Being a single mom
means teaching your children
that not all men leave.

•

836. Being a single mom
means wishing your mom
lived closer so she could baby-sit.

•

837. Being a single mom means
forgoing medical care for yourself
so you can afford it for your children.

•

838. Being a single mom means, at times,
putting your job ahead of your child
because you can't afford to lose it.

839. Being a single mom means trying to explain divorce. Without coming across as angry or on the verge of falling apart.

•

840. Being a single mom means worrying that your ex's new girlfriend could take your place in your child's heart.

•

841. Being a single mom means you're the one who has to say no.

842. Being a single mom means fighting to get child support. Sometimes, all the time.

•

843. Being a single mom means getting your degree because you don't want your child to grow up in poverty.

•

844. Being a single mom means realizing you're going to need the help of friends and relatives.

•

845. Being a single mom means you don't welcome random men into your house. Or your life.

846. Being a single mom means
coming to grips with the fact
your income will dive 45 percent
the first year after the divorce.

•

847. Being a single mom
means investigating to see
if flextime actually works.

•

848. Being a single mom means
trying to figure out how to maneuver
through the airport parking lot
while carrying a baby, tons of
baby stuff, suitcases, and a purse.

849. Being a single mom
means keeping a long list
of possible baby-sitters who
are available on short notice.

●

850. Being a single mom means
developing an inner resiliency:
your child needs to lean on you,
not have you lean on them.

●

851. Being a single mom means
writing a will. And telling baby-sitters
where to find important papers in
case something happens to you.

852. Being a single mom means knowing the average yearly cost to put two school-age children in day care before and after school, plus all day in the summer, is $13,490 a year.

•

853. Being a single mom means enrolling in your employer's MedFlex account.

•

854. Being a single mom means enforcing a bedtime curfew. For your kids' well-being. And your own.

855. Being a single mom means keeping to yourself your feelings about your kids' father.

•

856. Being a single mom means changing your plans. Frequently.

•

857. Being a single mom means developing a reciprocal pinch-hitting arrangement with a network of other moms.

•

858. Being a single mom means knowing that summer means two words: summer camp.

859. Being a single mom means
not setting your children up to
being left by one man after another.

•

860. Being a single mom means feeling
too tired to pray. But knowing you must.

•

861. Being a single mom
means practicing birth control.
Or odds are you'll have another
child in twenty-four months.

•

862. Being a single mom
means realizing the void in your
life can be filled only by God.

863. Being a single mom means understanding your family may be broken, but your home isn't.

•

864. Being a single mom means teaching your kids to not call strange men "Daddy."

•

865. Being a single mom means praying continuously, even though prayer doesn't come easily to a chronically exhausted person.

Moms
and Money

866. Being a mom means figuring out how to cut your grocery bill 40 percent after you quit work—even though you're adding another person to the family.

•

867. Being a mom means doing the math before returning to work. After child-care costs, commuting, taxes, and other expenses are tallied, you might not be earning as much as you think.

868. Being a mom means
having your kids
beg you for money.

•

869. Being a mom means
shopping at garage sales for baby
clothes because your child will
outgrow them in four weeks.

•

870. Being a mom means
buying things for your kids
even though you know your
husband is going to be upset.

871. Being a mom means
secretly wishing your
husband made more money.

•

872. Being a mom means
listening to other women
talking about vacationing in Maui
while you're trying to budget
for a plastic blow-up pool.

•

873. Being a mom means
teaching your kids that what you
are isn't based on what you have.

874. Being a mom means
constantly modeling how
money should be managed.

•

875. Being a mom means
monitoring your monthly expenses.

•

876. Being a mom means
having to say, "We can't afford it,"
no matter how much it kills you.

•

877. Being a mom means learning
to plan, to save, and to spend wisely.

878. Being a mom means worrying your kids don't have as many wonderful things as their friends do even though you know that's a stupid thing to worry about. But still...

•

879. Being a mom means weighing hiring a nanny versus enrolling in day care, maternity leave versus staying home, and private-school tuition versus a down payment on a home.

880. Being a mom means slipping your kids money when your husband isn't looking.

•

881. Being a mom means waking up to go to work while your kids sleep in. Even though they're younger, stronger, and healthier.

•

882. Being a mom means hearing about what all the other kids have when you can't afford those things for your own kids.

883. Being a mom means
finding your kids a job when
they seem unable to work up
the energy to even look.

•

884. Being a mom means
shopping at discount stores while
your kids look as if they stepped
off the pages of *Vogue* and *GQ*.

•

885. Being a mom means
forgetting you have a
budget at Christmastime.

886. Being a mom means
making dinner when
you'd rather go out.

•

**887. Being a mom means
realizing you need a will.**

•

888. Being a mom means
buying life insurance before
you conceive. (Insurance
companies now build in
the risks of postpartum
issues into their policies.)

889. Being a mom means deciding who will take care of your baby if you're not around.

•

890. Being a mom means starting a college fund.

•

891. Being a mom means feeling guilty about spending money on yourself.

Moms and
Difficult Issues

892. Being a mom means explaining to your kids that even though drugs are dangerous, you have a medicine cabinet full of them.

•

893. Being a mom means having your heart break when you realize your child is physically or mentally different from other kids. Yet, curiously, that difference makes you love them even more.

•

894. Being a mom means feeling lost when your child's behavioral problems are linked to a mental problem.

895. Being a mom means having your child evaluated because things don't seem to be going so well in school.

•

896. Being a mom means wondering if your child should really take ADD medicine every day. Then being even more alarmed when you understand how easy it is to abuse it.

•

897. Being a mom means realizing the last thing a child wants to be is "different."

898. Being a mom who has lost her husband redefines "lonely."

•

899. Being a widowed mom means the only people you can talk to at home are children.

•

900. Being a widowed mom means having to explain, through your tears, that Daddy is with God.

•

901. Being a widowed mom means showing your kids how to persevere even though life has dealt you a difficult hand.

902. Being a mom means trying
to make a troubled marriage
work for the sake of the kids.

•

903. Being a mom means agreeing to
family counseling for the kids' sake.

•

904. Being a mom means
getting along with a husband
you're divorcing especially when
you are around your children.

•

905. Being a mom means realizing
the inevitable effects of divorce on
children are longing, loss, and guilt.

906. Being a mom means
learning someone is bullying
your child and wanting the bully to
die. Even if he is only ten years old.

•

907. Being a mom means
teaching your child that bullies
don't pick on kids with friends.

•

908. Being a mom means
teaching and encouraging a
shy child how to make friends.

•

909. Being a mom means telling
your child how they should feel
even though you know that it never
works. You just want them to feel better.

910. Being a mom means teaching your kids—long before they start dating—to respect members of the opposite sex.

•

911. Being a mom means learning that the older children get, the more can go wrong.

•

912. Being a mom means always knowing what's going on in your child's life.

•

913. Being a mom means explaining to your kids how their world will end if they mess around with drugs, drinking, or sex.

914. Being a mom means
feeling a knife in your heart
whenever your child is rejected.

•

915. Being a mom means being
angry at the moms of the kids
who are mean to yours. You know
it's crazy, but you can't help it.

•

916. Being a mom means
remembering there are times
when teenagers can only express
themselves through anger. Even
though they've been taught otherwise.

917. Being a mom means being the kind of person you want your kids to be.

•

918. Being a mom means knowing kids aren't reasonable.

•

919. Being a mom means swallowing the sarcasm you want to use.

•

920. Being a mom means remembering you're teaching your daughter what it means to be a woman and teaching your son what to look for in a woman.

921. Being a mom means
not lying to your child.

•

922. Being a mom means
teaching your daughter to not
settle for Mr. Almost Right.

•

923. Being a mom means
teaching your children to take
responsibility for their actions.

•

924. Being a mom
means setting limits.

925. Being a mom means figuring out what your child is discouraged about.

•

926. Being a mom means not keeping alcohol in the house.

•

927. Being a mom means taking personally things like your kids' looks, grades, happiness, and success despite the glut of magazines, TV shows, and pop psychologists who say you shouldn't.

928. Being a mom means
feeling as if there's been a divorce
in the family when older kids fight.

•

**929. Being a mom means making
decisions that are difficult to make,
but are the best for your family.**

•

930. Being a mom means
searching for years for the
right therapist for your child.

931. Being a mom means
worrying that if your child
isn't gifted, he's disabled.
(Odds are very great he's neither.)

•

932. Being a mom means
feeling looked down upon
when your child misbehaves.

•

933. Being a mom means
feeling like a failure because
your child chooses to walk down
a rocky path in life. Even though
it's really a matter of them exercising
freedom of will and choice.

934. Being a mom means remembering four words: It's just a phase.

•

935. Being a mom means praying for a safer world for your children.

•

936. Being a mom means worrying that your child might one day have to go to war.

Moms and
Reading

BEING A MOM MEANS READING EVERYTHING YOU CAN GET YOUR HANDS ON. HERE IS A PRIMER LIST:

937. *What to Expect when You're Expecting* by Eisenberg, Murkoff, Eisenberg, and Hathaway

•

938. *What to Expect the First Year* by Eisenberg, Murkoff, and Hathaway

•

939. *What to Expect the Toddler Years* by Eisenberg, Murkoff, and Hathaway

940. *Dr. Spock's Baby and Child Care*
by Dr. Benjamin Spock

•

941. *Dr. Spock on Parenting*
by Dr. Benjamin Spock

•

942. *Toddler Taming*
by Dr. Christopher Green

•

943. *Your Baby and Child*
by Leach and Matthews

•

944. The New Strong-Willed Child
by Dr. James Dobson

945. *It Doesn't Take a Genius*
by McCutcheon and Lindsey

•

946. *Supernanny* by Jo Frost

•

947. *Positive Discipline*
by Jane Nelson

•

948. *The No-Cry Sleep Solution*
by Pantley and Sears

•

949. *Parenting with Love and Logic*
by Cline and Fay

950. *Real Boys* by Pollack and Piphar

•

951. *How to Talk so Kids Will Listen and Listen so Kids Will Talk* by Faber and Mazlish

•

952. *Raising a Self Starter* by Elizabeth Hartley-Brewer

•

953. *Touchpoints* by Brazelton and Sparrow

•

954. *Siblings Without Rivalry* by Faber, Mazlish, and Coe

955. *Raising Self-Reliant Children
in a Self-Indulgent World*
by Glenn and Nelson

•

956. *How to Help Your Child with
Homework* by Jeanne Schumm

•

957. *Parent Effectiveness Training* (PET)
by Thomas Gordon

•

958. *Why Gender Matters*
by Leonard Sax

959. *The Happiest Baby on the Block* by Harvey Karp

•

960. *Your Child's Self-Esteem* by Dorothy Briggs

•

961. *The Bully, the Bullied, and the Bystander* by Barbara Coloroso

•

962. *Rich Dad, Poor Dad* by Kiyosaki and Lecter

•

963. *What to Do...When Your Child Has Trouble at School* by Karen Levine

964. *Parents Are Teachers Too*
by Claudia Jones

•

965. *Walking on Eggshells*
by Jane Isay

•

966. *The Blessing of a Skinned Knee*
by Wendy Mogel

•

967. *The Pocket Parent*
by Reichlin and Winkler

•

968. *Grace-Based Parenting*
by Tim Kimmel

Moms and Grace

969. Being a mom means
recognizing that your
children are a gift from God.
And treating them as such.

•

970. Being a mom means
knowing fabulous clothes and
possessions won't make a
child happy or life meaningful.

•

971. Being a mom means
motivating the family
to go worship together.

972. Being a mom means making time for your husband.

•

973. Being a mom means encouraging your children to be noble.

•

974. Being a mom means reading the Bible every morning.

•

975. Being a mom means being consistent.

976. Being a mom means
silently thanking God for
piles of dirty laundry and all the
toys lying on the kitchen floor.

•

977. Being a mom means
teaching a child to see
the wonder in each day.

•

978. Being a mom
means treasuring the
simple things in life.

979. Being a mom means
showing your kids how
the rest of the world lives.

•

980. Being a mom means
teaching your kids that
certain things in life are
worth sacrificing for.

•

981. Being a mom means
believing in miracles. And
wishing they'd come quicker.

982. Being a mom means
experiencing moments of great
beauty, amazing tenderness,
sticky kisses, and a miracle
or two—all in a single day.

•

983. Being a mom means
finding other mothers
who will pray for you.

•

984. Being a mom means
teaching that the past is history
and the future is a mystery.
And that all we have is the present.

985. Being a mom means realizing you can't make your kids become who you want them to be, but you can help them become who they're meant to be.

•

986. Being a mom means devoting yourself to your child. It's what mothers do.

•

987. Being a mom means treasuring every day God lets you have your child.

988. Being a mom means you're happiest when you're surrounded by your family.

•

989. Being a mom means praying that you live long enough to watch your children grow up.

•

990. Being a mom means thanking God for this experience.

•

991. Being a mom means making each of your children feel special.

992. Being a mom means
teaching your kids that sex is
a gift from God for a husband
and wife, so it's not to be trifled
with outside of marriage.

•

**993. Being a mom means
realizing your children
aren't your confidants.**

•

994. Being a mom means
cultivating compassion in your child
by being compassionate yourself.

995. Being a mom means
teaching a child to hope.

•

996. Being a mom means forgiving
your children before they ask.

•

997. Being a mom means
trying to make everything perfect.
And being upset when you can't.

•

998. Being a mom means
teaching your children to pray.

999. Being a mom means
loving your husband even more
after having children because
of the love he has for them.

•

1000. Being a mom
means never giving up.

•

1001. Being a mom means
knowing childhood ends
but motherhood never does.